This edition published 2005 by
Mercury Books
20 Bloomsbury Street
London WC1B 3JH
ISBN 1-904668-76-3
Copyright © 2003 Allegra Publishing Ltd

Publisher: Felicia Law
Design director: Tracy Carrington
Project manager: Karen Foster
Author: Gerry Bailey
Editor: Rosalind Beckman
Designed by: Jacqueline Palmer
assisted by Simon Brewster, Will Webster
Cartoon illustrations: Steve Boulter (Advocate)
Make-and-do: Jan Smith
Model-maker: Tim Draper
Photo studio: Steve Lumb
Photo research: Diana Morris
Scanning: Imagewrite
Digital workflow: Edward MacDermott

Printed by D 2 Print Singapore

Crafty Inventions

OUTER SPACE

Contents

Mercury Junior

20 BLOOMSBURY STREET
LONDON WC1B 3JH

Can a satellite orbit the Earth?

For thousands of years, astronomers have studied the planets and noted how they orbit the Sun. They also discovered that the Moon orbits the Earth. An artificial body, or satellite, that goes round the Earth could send back useful information. Is a satellite in space possible?

Even if scientists send a satellite into space, how can they get it to stay in orbit around the Earth? And how do they get it up there in the first place?

A rocket is the only form of transport that will work. But it would have to be powerful enough to carry the extra weight of the satellite.

Russian scientists are working on a special project called Sputnik, which means 'traveller' in Russian. It's a type of transmitter that can gather information from space and send it back to Earth by radio signal.

What can we use to send a satellite into space – and keep it there?

WHAT DID THEY DO?

- Russian technicians built a two-stage space vehicle that could fly fast enough to get it and a small payload into space.

- Scientists discovered that an artificial satellite will stay in orbit if there is a balance between its straight line speed and the pull of Earth's gravity on it.

- A base on Earth was constructed to receive the radio signal data from the space transmitter.

- The transmitter, cased in a metal sphere, was fitted to the spacecraft that carried it into orbit. All of this was done in utmost secrecy.

We know that at 933km above the Earth's surface, the speed of Sputnik will balance the force of gravity by trying to pull it back to Earth. It will stay fixed at that height, orbiting the planet every 96 minutes.

The Russian satellite Sputnik 1 was the first man-made object put into space.

Obtaining data

An **artificial satellite** is any spacecraft launched into **orbit** around the Earth or any other planet. Sputnik 1 was the world's first artificial satellite. It went into orbit on 4 October 1957. Thousands of satellites have been launched since then, including Telstar. Launched by the US in 1962, Telstar sent live television pictures across the Atlantic for the first time.

Satellites have a wide range of uses, including astronomical experiments and observations, communications, remote sensing, weather forecasting and military reconnaissance. Most artificial satellites are unmanned but some, like the Russian Vostok missions of the 1960s, have an **astronaut** or **cosmonaut** aboard to carry out scientific experiments.

In orbit

An orbit is the path of one body around another in space. Artificial satellites orbit other bodies in space, just as natural satellites do.

There are three main types of satellite orbit. A high altitude **geosynchronous orbit** allows the satellite to stay in a position fixed above a certain spot on Earth all the time. The satellite, which is 35,900km above the planet, travels around the Earth's **axis** in the same time and in the same direction as the Earth rotates. Because of this, it looks as if it isn't moving. A **polar orbit** passes over the north and south poles, but always crosses the Equator at the same time of day. As it flies over all latitudes, it can gather data on all parts of the Earth. A **low Earth orbit** is about 300km above Earth. The space shuttle and the MIR space station orbit at this lower level.

SPACE JUNK

What happens when a satellite has finished doing its job? Is it possible that space may become littered with out-of-date, useless satellites? Actually, most satellites slow down, lose their orbits and are pulled back towards Earth. Then they burn up in the atmosphere. But if they don't - watch out!

A satellite in a geosynchronous orbit can relay telecommunications data such as telephone calls.

Inventor's words

artificial satellite
astronaut • axis
cosmonaut
geosynchronous orbit
low Earth orbit
orbit
polar orbit

Make an alien satellite

You will need

- balloon • newspaper
- PVA glue
- thick cardboard
- string • kebab sticks
- scissors and craft knife
- paints and brush
- glitter glue pens
- metallic stars, glitter
- wire • pen
- clay or plasticine

1 To make a planet, blow up a large, round balloon and cover it with layers of newspaper strips soaked in glue and water. Allow to dry.

2 Tie some string to a piece of kebab stick. Make a hole in the top of the planet and push the stick through. Pull back the string (the stick will lock it in place).

3 Cut a star-shape into the top of your planet and pull out the segments to form a crater. Decorate with a mixture of paint and glue, and sprinkle on glitter and stars before it dries.

4 Cut out a cardboard ring that will fit over your planet. Decorate with paint and stripes of glitter glue.

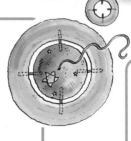

5 Push 4 kebab sticks into the inner circle of the ring. Then hold the ring around the middle of the planet and mark the position of the sticks with a pen. Make small holes where the marks are and slot in the ring. Glue to secure.

6 Make a plasticine alien and pop him into the crater.

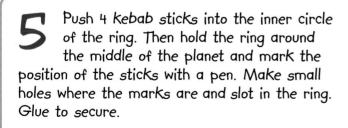

Hang your satellite by a window and watch it spin!

How can we send a man into space?

Getting a rocket high into the atmosphere and then into space is amazing. But that's just the beginning. Now scientists want to send a man into space, or even to the Moon. This will take a huge amount of power and thrust. A single rocket doesn't have enough of either.

Robert Goddard built the first liquid-propelled rocket in 1926. It didn't go very high. But the idea had exciting possibilities.

Further experiments were carried out by scientists in the Soviet Union, America and Germany. The German V2 of World War II worked brilliantly.

After the war, Americans took German scientists and their V2s back to America. But the rockets were not powerful enough for space travel. They were too slow and too heavy, because they needed to carry huge quantities of fuel.

What we need is a super-light, extra-powerful rocket!

WHAT DID THEY DO?

- The US Navy worked on a rocket programme and came up with the Aerobee and Viking rockets.

- These were fine for military use. But something much more powerful was needed for space exploration.

- In 1903, Konstantin Tsiolkovsky, a Russian scientist, had made an important observation. He suggested a multi-section, or stage, rocket would work better than a single-stage one.

- The Russians put a satellite in space using their R-7 rocket. It had two stages. Was this the answer to expanding space exploration?

Multi-stage rockets are the answer! Each stage carries its own engine and propellant. When the fuel is used up, the stage falls off. This lightens the rocket and makes it faster. The second stage then fires. A third stage would make the rocket even faster.

Saturn lifts off on its final mission to the orbiting space station, Skylab 4.

Fast and light

A **multi-stage rocket** is made up of two or more sections called stages. Each stage has a rocket engine and a **propellant**, or fuel mix. Multi-stage rockets were developed because single-stage rockets could not reach high enough speeds to make space exploration feasible. A multi-stage rocket lightens its weight by dropping each stage as it uses up its propellant.

This makes it faster. A three-stage rocket, for example, can reach about three times the speed of a single-stage rocket, using the same amount of fuel. The first stage, called a **booster**, launches the rocket. After it has burned off all its fuel, it is dropped and the second stage takes over. This process continues using one stage after another until they are all used up.

Combustion

Rocket fuel is a special mixture of chemicals that are burned in a combustion chamber. The combustion, or burning, causes the gas that forms to expand rapidly and flow out of the rear of the rocket. The rocket is pushed forward by an equal force acting on the top of the chamber.

If combustion is all that is needed, why not simply use a big petrol engine, or even a jet engine? The problem is that combustion cannot happen without oxygen. Petrol engines and jet engines get their oxygen from the air in the atmosphere. But they wouldn't work in space where there is no atmosphere. Rocket engines carry oxygen with them in the form of an **oxidiser**. The oxidiser is mixed with the fuel in the combustion chamber. Liquid fuel rockets, like Saturn, carry tanks of liquid oxygen that is mixed with fuels such as liquid hydrogen.

ATOMIC ROCKETS?

Some scientists think an atomic reactor could be used to power a rocket, as it would create more energy than a chemical engine. However, as the reactor would be radioactive, it would need a thick protective shield. That would make the rocket too heavy to lift off the ground.

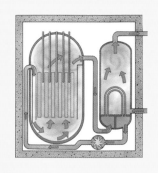

A liquid fuel system usually uses pumps and valves to get the chemicals to the combustion chamber.

Inventor's words

booster
combustion
multi-stage rocket
oxidiser
propellant
rocket fuel

Make a three-stage rocket

You will need

- glue tube nozzle
- plastic bottle tops • corks
- PVA glue • card
- scissors and craft knife
- 3 cardboard tubes: large, medium, small
- double-sided sticky tape
- string • wires
- corrugated metallic card
- holographic tape,
- double-sided tape
- paints and brush

1 Make the rocket nozzle by sticking together a glue tube nozzle, bottle tops and a cork.

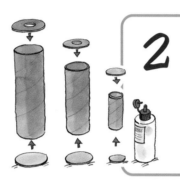

2 Cut 6 cardboard discs to fit over the ends of the 3 cardboard tubes. Now cut cork-sized holes into the top discs before you glue them down.

3 Glue corks under the bases of the small and medium tube. Then make a set of card wing flaps to stick on each tube.

4 To make a rocket thruster, glue together 2 bottle tops and a cork and wrap sticky tape around the bottle tops before winding string around them. Stick 5 of these to the base of the largest tube.

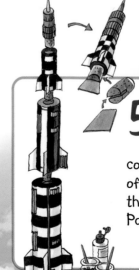

5 Mount your rocket by slotting the corks on the base of each tube into the section below. Paint and decorate.

Break away

How can we travel into space?

Scientists have dreamed of travelling in space ever since the first rockets were invented. But how is it possible to get someone safely to a place with no atmosphere, no gravity and a lot of dangerous particles flying about? It's also a long way to the nearest stopping point - the Moon.

Because there is no air in space, there is no oxygen to breathe. The temperature can be very low or very high, depending on whether or not you are facing the Sun.

A huge force will be needed to get a spacecraft off the ground and into space. It may be too great for humans to survive.

How can we get someone safely into space and back again?

Returning to Earth will be as dangerous as getting into space. The re-entry speed will be so great, the spacecraft will heat up to thousands of degrees. Landing must be gentle enough not to kill the astronauts on contact.

WHAT DID THEY DO?

- Adding a cockpit from a fighter plane to a V2 rocket might help. But a single-stage rocket wouldn't be powerful enough.

- They could build a three-stage rocket and put the astronaut somewhere inside the third stage. Powerful rocket - but no good for the astronaut!

- If they attached a plane-type cockpit to the rocket, it might just stay in place when blasted into space. Unlikely!

- How about a separate cone structure above the third stage, with a parachute system to slow it down when it returns to Earth?

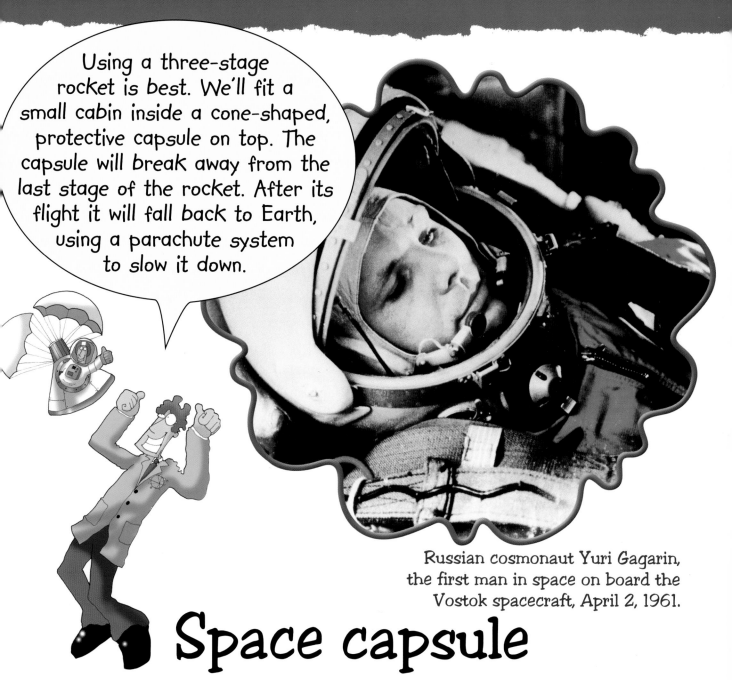

Using a three-stage rocket is best. We'll fit a small cabin inside a cone-shaped, protective capsule on top. The capsule will break away from the last stage of the rocket. After its flight it will fall back to Earth, using a parachute system to slow it down.

Russian cosmonaut Yuri Gagarin, the first man in space on board the Vostok spacecraft, April 2, 1961.

Space capsule

A **space capsule** is a tiny pressurised cabin perched on top of a multi-stage rocket. The early capsules contained just enough room for the **cosmonaut** or **astronaut**, who sat in an ejection seat. The seat would eject if there was a problem on launching. Once the rocket had gathered enough speed, the capsule was released.

The first **space** flights orbiting Earth lasted from 15 minutes to two hours. When the capsule plunged back into the Earth's atmosphere, the astronaut was protected from the heat by an outer shield. At a precise height, parachutes were released to slow it down. Soviet capsules touched down on land; American ones landed in the sea.

Space

Space is everything that lies outside, or beyond, our Earth and its atmosphere. It includes many objects such as the planets, stars, gas clouds and black holes.

The space just above Earth is called **outer space**. There is no definite boundary but astronomers have fixed it at about 95km above our planet. Space isn't empty. It contains particles of air, space dust, stone or metallic chunks called meteoroids, and all kinds of radiation, including gamma rays. The space between planets is called **interplanetary space**. Vast distances separate the planets and the Sun. Earth, for example, is 150 million km from the Sun. **Interstellar space** is the space between stars. It contains many strange objects, including gas clouds. Distances between stars are so great, they are measured in **light years**, or how far light travels in a year, which is over 9 trillion km.

FIRST ROCKETS

The Chinese used the first rockets when they fired 'arrows of flying fire' against Mongol invaders in 1232. But it wasn't until the 1880s that military rockets were invented by the British army to carry explosives. These were developed into the high-powered rockets we know today.

Interstellar space contains some spectacular gas clouds. This eerie, dark 'nebula' is an incubator for new stars.

Inventor's words

astronaut • black holes
cosmonaut
interplanetary space
interstellar space
light year
outer space
space capsule

Make an Apollo lander

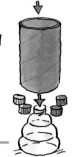

You will need

- scissors or craft knife
- bottle tops • cardboard
- cardboard tubes
- plastic bottles • PVA glue
- corrugated card
- egg carton
- double-sided sticky tape
- small boxes • kebab sticks
- tinfoil cake dishes
- silver and white paints
- metallic tape and holographic stickers
- paints and brush

1 To make the Apollo module, glue together the top end of a small plastic bottle, a cardboard disc, a cardboard tube and a large plastic bottle top, as shown. Decorate with bottle tops and corrugated card.

2 To make the lander module, glue together the top end of a small plastic bottle, a piece of egg carton and a large plastic bottle top, as shown. Tape a small box to each side and stick on bottle tops.

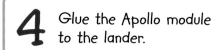

3 Push 4 kebab stick legs into the egg carton base and glue on tinfoil dishes for landing feet. Make and attach a cardboard ladder.

4 Glue the Apollo module to the lander.

5 Paint and decorate with foil dishes, metallic tape and holographic stickers.

15

What shall we wear in space?

When astronauts and cosmonauts were clothed for space, they weren't too fussed about the latest fashion. The main issue was safety. But safety from what? Well, heat and cold for a start. But those weren't the only problems...

Special clothing is worn by the pilots who fly jet aircraft to keep them warm at high altitudes. If oxygen is low, an oxygen mask helps the pilots to breathe.

Astronauts also need special clothing. But they require extra protection, especially for when they leave the spacecraft.

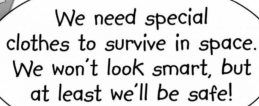

We need special clothes to survive in space. We won't look smart, but at least we'll be safe!

Potential space walkers are faced with dangers never before encountered. There will be no oxygen for breathing; temperatures change dramatically from freezing to boiling; and dangerous radiation will be a constant hazard.

WHAT DID THEY DESIGN?

- The suit had to be airtight, but it needed to be flexible, too, so that the astronaut could move about easily.

- Strong materials were essential for the various parts of the outfit.

- A warm suit wasn't enough. A cooling system needed to be fitted into the suit material as well.

- Helmets had to offer good visibility. But they also had to protect the astronauts from harmful radiation.

- A supply of oxygen was vital, and carbon dioxide and moisture had to be easily removed.

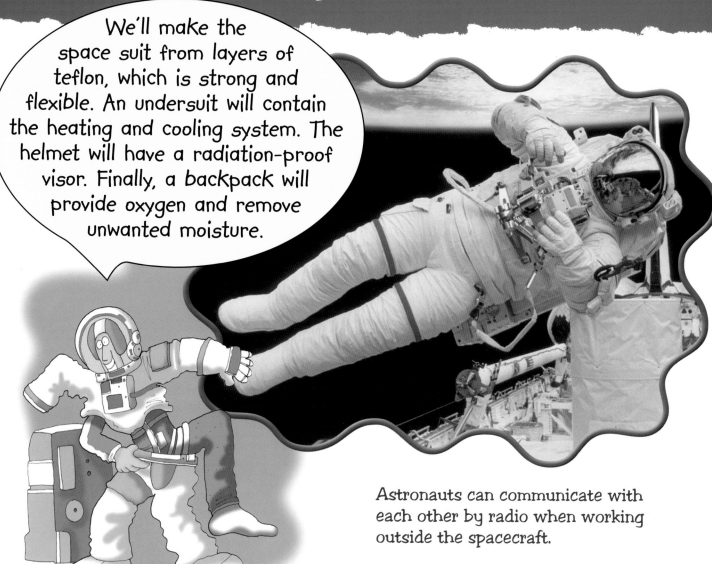

We'll make the space suit from layers of teflon, which is strong and flexible. An undersuit will contain the heating and cooling system. The helmet will have a radiation-proof visor. Finally, a backpack will provide oxygen and remove unwanted moisture.

Astronauts can communicate with each other by radio when working outside the spacecraft.

Getting dressed

A **space suit** is a double garment worn by astronauts. The outer covering of the space suit protects the astronaut from harmful radiation and from space particles. The **undersuit**, or inner suit, contains the heating and cooling systems that protect against very hot or very cold temperatures. Gloves must be flexible as well as warm.

These allow astronauts to hold small objects and work with tools outside the spacecraft. A helmet protects against radiation and glare. The backpack provides oxygen for the astronaut to breathe and removes harmful carbon dioxide and moisture. A space suit can keep an astronaut alive in a hostile environment for up to eight hours.

Space walk

A walk in space is known as extra-vehicular activity, or EVA. The first person to do this was a cosmonaut from the Soviet Union, in 1965. He went outside his spacecraft, Voskhod 2, for 10 minutes. Since then, many cosmonauts and astronauts have left their spacecraft to make repairs or to explore.

Before leaving the spacecraft, astronauts must put on their space suit. The undersuit goes on first, then the bottom half of the oversuit. Next, they slip into the top half of the oversuit, which hangs from a wall bracket. The two halves of the suit are joined together with tight mechanical seals. Finally, they put on heavy boots, gloves and a helmet. The backpack is then attached to the suit. The first astronauts were connected to the spacecraft by life-lines, but now a manned manoeuvring unit, or **MMU**, is used.

SAFE ATTACHMENT

The MMU is a one-man propulsion backpack that allows astronauts to make space walks unconnected to the spacecraft. It is powered by jets of nitrogen gas. First used in 1984, the MMU allows astronauts to move about 90m from the orbiter.

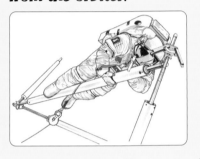

An astronaut puts on his undersuit in preparation for an EVA.

Inventor's words

astronaut
cosmonaut
EVA · MMU
orbiter
space suit
undersuit

Make an astro-helmet

You will need

- bendable wire, thin and thick
- double-sided sticky tape
- scissors • card
- PVA glue • wire cutters
- masking tape • newspaper
- black, white and silver paints, brush • small boxes
- foil tubs
- metallic tapes

1 Use thick bendable wire to make 6 same-size loops with an open bottom. Make sure they fit over your head with room to spare.

2 Bind the wire loops together with tape. Cut out a strip of card and tape around the base of the loops to make a collar.

3 Weave the thin wire in and out of the 6 loops to make a strong framework. Glue over every join in the wires and allow to dry.

4 Using wire cutters, cut a wide hole into the front of the helmet. Cover the helmet in masking tape and lay on strips of newspaper soaked in glue and water. When dry, paint the helmet with a black undercoat.

5 Glue on a visor-shaped piece of card above the visor hole and add boxes and foil tubs for ear phones. Paint the outside of your astro-helmet white and silver, and decorate with strips of metallic tape.

How can we travel on the Moon?

When Apollo 11 blasted off for the Moon in 1969, the main aim was to show the first man walking on the surface of another world. Only two experiments were carried out. The mission was a success, but later explorations wanted to carry out more detailed investigations.

Astronauts look odd as they bounce along on the surface of the Moon. With much less gravity to pull them down, they don't weigh as much as they do on Earth.

This means they can jump further in the air. But it's tiring to move too far away from the lunar module, so they only carry out experiments close by.

As scientists decide that they need more information on the Moon and its surface, the astronauts need to travel further away from the module. But it can't be done on foot. Some kind of vehicle is needed.

How can we carry out all our experiments without wearing ourselves out?

WHAT DID THEY DO?

- They couldn't use a car, because cars have petrol engines that use oxygen from the air. And there's no air on the Moon.

- A vehicle with a sail is no use either, because there's no atmosphere on the Moon. So there's no wind to power the sail.

- Wheels with tyres can't be used. The tyres would explode because there's no air pressure.

- And then there's weight to consider. The vehicle would have to be light enough to take on the journey, and small enough to fold away at the side of the Lunar module.

A lightweight 'buggy' will work best. Each wheel will be powered by a small engine, using electricity from batteries. We'll use strong wire to make the wheels. Finally, we must check it will be strong enough to withstand blast-off.

The lunar rover could carry two astronauts plus their life support systems and scientific instruments. Its longest single journey was 20km.

Driving in space

A **lunar roving vehicle**, or rover, was designed to make journeys across the surface of the **Moon**. It was powered by electric motors, which fed four $1/4$-horsepower engines at each wheel. It weighed about 209kg on the Moon, and could carry a total payload of 490 Earth kilograms.

As ordinary wheels and tyres couldn't be used, special wheels were made out of woven piano wire. The rear wheels steered the lunar rover. All three rovers used had a top speed of 13km per hour. Astronauts made criss-cross journeys, travelling up to 7.6km away from the lunar module.

The Moon

The Moon is Earth's satellite and the only other body in space that humans have walked on. The Moon orbits the Earth every 27 days, 7 hours and 43 minutes. It rotates on its axis at about the same speed, so just one side of the Moon is ever visible in the night sky. Only when a Russian spacecraft orbited the Moon and took pictures of it, did we see what the other side looked like.

Scientists have different theories as to why the Moon exists. Many believe the **splash theory**, that Earth was hit early in its history by a huge object. Material splashed from the Earth's molten surface to create a ring around it. The debris of the ring then **coalesced**, or joined together, to create the Moon. Other ideas are that the Moon was formed from dust around the Earth when the Earth itself was forming, or that it was captured by Earth's gravity.

MOON GLASS

The lunar rover allowed astronauts to travel further afield to find rock samples. One interesting find was a type of orange soil. When it was analysed, it was found to contain ancient coloured particles of glass.

The Moon's surface is covered in pulverised rock. Its features include impact craters, volcanic craters, lava flows and fault lines.

Inventor's words

axis
coalesce
lunar roving
vehicle
Moon • orbit
splash theory

Make a moon mobil

You will need

- scissors and craft knife
- 3 toilet roll tubes
- pencil • polystyrene
- PVA glue • kebab sticks
- card, cardboard
- small cardboard boxes
- plastic lids • pipecleaners
- straws • bottle tops
- corrugated and holographic card, foil
- copper wires
- paints and brush

1 Cut the toilet roll tubes in half to make 6 wheels. Draw round the end of a tube and cut out 6 card discs. Stick a disc over one end of each wheel.

2 Stick a lump of polystyrene inside each wheel. Use 3 kebab sticks for the axles and push a wheel onto one end of each stick. Glue to fix.

3 Punch 3 evenly-spaced holes into a thick bar of cardboard. Thread the axles through the holes and fix the other wheels in place.

4 Build the main body from small boxes glued together and plastic lids.

5 Thread pipe cleaners through straws to make 3 probe-arms: bend one arm into a claw; attach another to a bottle top for a suction pad; stick on a piece of shiny card for a solar panel. Wind on copper wire.

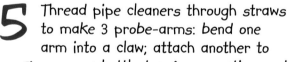

6 Fix probes to the main body. Paint and decorate.

How can we explore outer space?

Compared to vehicles on Earth, manned spacecraft move very quickly. But if you consider the distances between planets, actually they are very slow. A spacecraft could take years to reach a planet and more than a lifetime to reach the stars. There must be a quicker way to explore space.

Before astronauts and cosmonauts travelled into space, unmanned vehicles were used to discover what conditions were like beyond Earth's atmosphere.

The first attempts to explore the atmosphere and beyond were made in the 1940s. Sounding rockets carried instruments and took photographs of Earth.

How can we get information on outer space without having to wait years and years?

But no one thought of them as real spacecraft. It wasn't until 1957 and the launch of the Russian satellite, Sputnik, that the true Space Age began. Still, just how far into space people could explore, no one knew.

WHAT DID THEY DO?

● Scientists wanted to find out what space was like between the Earth and the Moon. They also wanted to study the Moon up close.

● In the 1950s and 1960s, US Explorer satellites and USSR Kosmos satellites analysed near space. Then the USSR sent Luna probes to try to learn more about the Moon.

● Luna 2 hit the Moon. Luna 3 did even better. It orbited the Moon and sent back pictures of the far side – the first time it had ever been seen.

● Further probes returned with lunar soil samples and collected information that would one day help a manned flight to the Moon.

24

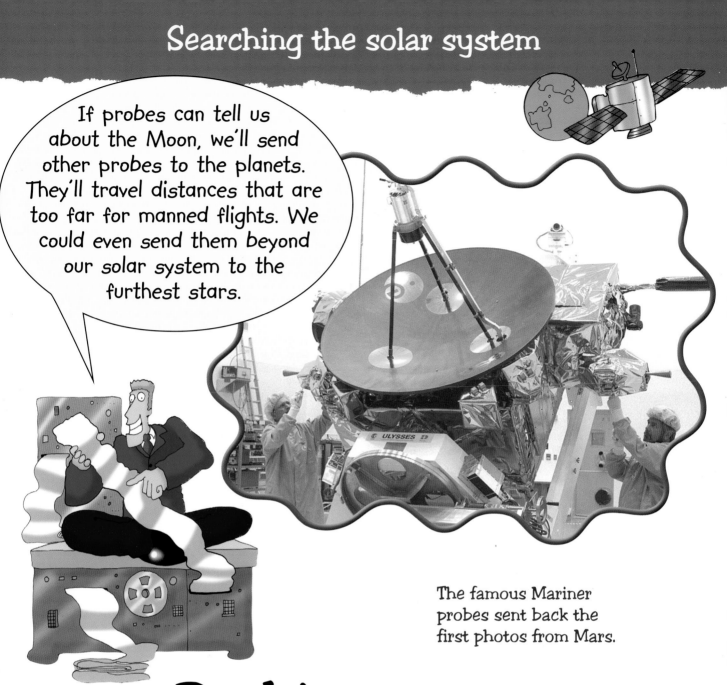

If probes can tell us about the Moon, we'll send other probes to the planets. They'll travel distances that are too far for manned flights. We could even send them beyond our solar system to the furthest stars.

The famous Mariner probes sent back the first photos from Mars.

Probing space

A **space probe** is an unmanned space flight. Probes carry out missions to find out about moons, planets and other objects in the **solar system**. They may operate far out in space or land on moons or planets. Probes can carry instruments to observe objects in space, take temperatures or measure radiation. Some actually land on their targets.

There, instruments take samples from the surface, measure the density of the atmosphere or photograph the terrain. These probes are called soft landers, because they land gently. The first probes were known as impact vehicles, because they didn't slow down before landing. Their penetrators rammed deeply into a planet to take specimens.

Planet power

Space probes use different kinds of power to get them into space. Rocket power is often used to carry probes into **orbit** or towards the Moon. While in space, probes may use solar power, or the power from the Sun's heat, to push them along. Once in deep space, probes sometimes use nuclear power to keep them going.

At one point, however, the two Voyager probes used a different sort of power – planet power. The probes used the gravity of the giant planet Jupiter to increase their speed and shoot them off towards Saturn and beyond. As each probe closed in on the huge planet, Jupiter's massive **gravitation** began to pull on it, thereby increasing its speed. When the Voyagers passed Jupiter, this extra speed worked to catapult them off in the direction of Saturn. Scientists gauged how Jupiter's gravity could be used before the probes took off.

ALIEN PROBE

When the Voyager craft finished their visits to the far planets, they headed out into deep space. At some point in the future, scientists believe they might be found by an alien race. So each Voyager probe carries a record player and records with sounds of Earth, and pictures of people.

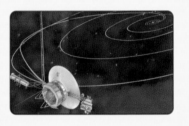

The Voyager probes passed by Saturn and its moons on their way across the solar system.

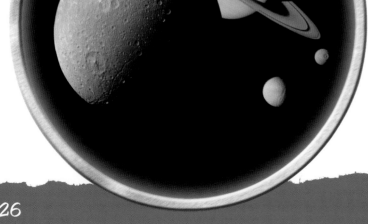

Inventor's words

gravitation
orbit
penetrators
solar system
space probe

Make a UFO

You will need
- thin card • scissors
- 2 large foil pie dishes
- sticky tape • PVA glue
- kebab sticks • buttons
- metallic card
- toilet roll tube • marbles
- clay or plasticine
- paints and brush
- pieces of wire scourer
- plastic bottle
- old coins or small card discs covered in tin foil
- glitter, sweets

1 To make the UFO body, stick a strip of card around the top of one pie dish with tape. Then stick the other dish on top. Cover with newspaper strips soaked in glue.

2 Push 3 sticks into the base of the craft for the legs. Glue on landing feet made from buttons stuck to squares of metallic card. Stick a piece of toilet roll underneath.

3 Make 2 marble-eyed plasticine aliens, one full figure, the other head-only.

4 Glue the alien head to the top of the UFO and cover with the bottom half of a plastic bottle to make a cockpit. Glue to fix.

5 Make a transporter beam by cutting out a triangle of metallic card and fixing the tab to the toilet roll base.

6 Decorate the UFO with paint, glitter, wire, tin foil discs, and sweets for spotlights.

Can we recycle a spacecraft?

Rocket scientists have come a long way since the days of single-stage spacecraft. Now they produce powerful multi-stage rockets. The trouble is, these huge spacecraft are very expensive and they can only be used once. Is it possible to find a cheaper alternative?

Every time an Apollo spacecraft heads into space, it costs millions of dollars. Space authorities are worried that the cost is getting out of hand.

If rockets could be used more than once, it would save money. It would also be more efficient.

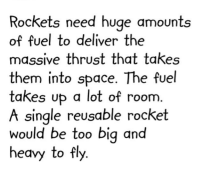

Rockets need huge amounts of fuel to deliver the massive thrust that takes them into space. The fuel takes up a lot of room. A single reusable rocket would be too big and heavy to fly.

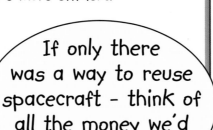

If only there was a way to reuse spacecraft - think of all the money we'd save!

WHAT DID THEY NEED?

- A reusable spacecraft must be able to land back on Earth, so it would need wings for gliding.

- It would also require rockets to allow it to make adjustments to its movement in space.

- Somehow, it must be able to withstand the incredible heat generated when it re-enters the Earth's atmosphere.

- Space is important, too. There must be enough room to store all the materials it will need, such as satellites and building materials. But despite this huge payload, the spacecraft must have enormous power.

A winged rocket 'plane' that can glide on to an airstrip will work. It will ride piggyback on a huge external fuel tank. Reusable rocket boosters attached to the tank will provide extra power. Ceramic tiles will protect it from high temperatures.

Photo of the Orbiter Challenger, taken with a camera aboard the Shuttle Pallet Satellite.

A fleet of shuttles

A **space shuttle** is a spacecraft built by the United States of America. It can be reused many times, unlike three-stage rockets. Space shuttles are launched like rockets, but they can land like an aircraft on a runway. The winged **orbiter** sits on top of a large cigar-shaped fuel tank. It gets extra power from two solid fuel **booster rockets** that are strapped to the sides of the tank.

When the boosters have done their job, they fall back to Earth and can be used again. Later on, the fuel tank is also jettisoned. Now, just the orbiter itself is left to do its job, using small engines to move about. On its return, ceramic tiles protect it from the huge temperatures it encounters when re-entering the Earth's atmosphere, before it finally glides to a landing at an airfield.

Space shuttle

A space shuttle is designed to act as a kind of space workhorse. It can be used over and over again to do a variety of different jobs. In the nose of the orbiter is the pressurised cabin, where the pilot sits. Below is a middeck, which contains seats for mission specialists. It's their job to oversee the shuttle's objective.

An **airlock** leads from the middeck to the **payload bay**, where all the materials needed to carry out the spacecraft's mission are stored. The shuttle programme included many different kinds of mission. Commercial satellite launches began in 1982. During the 1980s, top secret military missions were carried out. Another important function is the carrying out of repairs. The Hubble telescope was successfully corrected in 1993. The shuttle also carries spacelab, a manned laboratory in space that carries out many important experiments.

MASHED MOLECULES

Many people believe a spacecraft's skin is heated by friction when it enters the Earth's atmosphere. Well, they are wrong! At such great speeds air cannot move out of the way of the spacecraft fast enough. The molecules of air pile up in front of it and become compressed, or mashed together. This squeezing causes the air to heat up to over 5000° C.

Repair work on the free-flying Solar Maximum Satellite is carried out during a shuttle mission.

Inventor's words

airlock
booster rockets
middeck
mission specialist
molecules
orbiter
payload bay
space shuttle

Make a 3-D solar system

You will need

- thick cardboard
- scissors or craft knife
- pencil
- reference book on space
- tissue paper
- PVA glue • tissue paper
- poster paints and brush
- pipe cleaners, straws
- stick-on stars, glitter

1 Cut out a large panel of cardboard. Next, cut out 9 planet discs (use your book to check the sizes).

2 Draw the Sun as a big half circle on the left hand side of the panel and glue on the planets in order from left to right.

3 Build up the larger planets in 3-D by cutting out more discs and gluing them on top of each other in size order, finishing with the smallest on top.

4 Using tissue paper soaked in PVA glue and water, cover the discs, moulding the planets into smooth spheres. Also build up a mound along the outer edge of the Sun.

5 Cut out a cardboard ring, then cut a piece out and glue it in place around Saturn.

6 Use paint and tissue paper to decorate your solar system. Use pipe cleaners and straws for planetary trajectories, and add stick-on stars and glitter for an outer space effect.

How can I see far into space?

Early astronomers used the naked eye to view the stars. When telescopes were invented, they became the astronomer's most important tool. Telescopes gather lightwaves to make an image of phenomena in space. But there's a limit to how much can be seen through them.

Many new and exciting telescopes have been built around the world, and astronomers can *see* stars and star systems more clearly than ever before.

But they know there is more to be seen and discovered. Unfortunately, they have to rely on light that is coming from huge distances away. The images are unclear.

But is light the only thing radiating from space? Engineer Karl Jansky has been getting static interference with radio messages, which he can't identify. They appear four minutes earlier each day. Very odd!

I wonder where these static radio waves are coming from. They could be very useful...

WHAT DID HE DO?

- Jansky knew that the stars also rise four minutes earlier each day. So he reckoned that the radio signals were coming from stars beyond our solar system.

- Jansky was correct. In 1931, he discovered that radio waves radiate from outer space.

- Astronomers didn't make use of the discovery immediately. But Grote Reber, another American engineer, built a bowl-shaped radio telescope in his back yard.

- A few years later, other astronomers took up the idea. They used radio waves to study objects in space, just as they had used lightwaves.

A telescope that gathers radio waves will have a reflector dish the same shape as an optical telescope's mirror. The dish will focus the waves on to an antenna. The waves will be turned into electrical signals, which can be used to draw a picture of the object in space.

Radio telescopes pick up strong sources of radio waves from the Sun and the centres of galaxies.

Radio waves

Radio telescopes are used to collect radio signals from space. They are very large because radio waves are longer than lightwaves. Most radio telescopes use a dish antenna to receive the waves. Motors turn the dish towards the source of the radio waves, which might be a star or galaxy. The radio waves are changed into electrical signals.

These are amplified, or made stronger, by a radio receiver. The receiver then records their strength and frequency, or the number of radio waves per second, as data on a tape. A computer analyses the data and draws a picture of the source of the radio waves. It can also analyse the **radio spectrum** and chemical make-up of the source.

Deepest space

Radio telescopes have allowed astronomers to find the truth about some of the mysteries of deep space. They discovered that the giant clouds of gas that exist between stars give out regular pulses of radio waves. They learned too that dark, star-like objects they couldn't identify also radiated huge amounts of radio waves. The clouds they called pulsars; the dark objects are known as quasars.

A pulsar is a piece of matter left over from the explosion of a **supernova**. It spins around rapidly in space and, as it does so, it gives off beams of radio waves. The waves seem to switch on and off as the pulsar passes across the Earth. A quasar is a **galaxy** with a bright centre, which is far out in space. As well as visible light, quasars send out strong radio signals. The signals we receive left the quasar millions of years ago.

MAP MAKER

How do scientists map a planet they've never visited? They use a radio telescope, which acts as a giant radar system. Radio waves are sent to the planet from the telescope. They bounce back and the echo is recorded as different electrical signals. A computer uses these signals to draw the map.

This image of the Crab Nebula shows a faint object at its centre, identified as a pulsar, which is thought to be the remains of the original star.

Inventor's words

amplify • galaxy
pulsar • quasar
radio spectrum
radio telescope
supernova

Make a radar

You will need
- wok or shallow bowl
- food wrap
- newspaper • PVA glue
- plastic bottles
- bendable wire
- paint and brush
- bottle tops
- thin cardboard tube
- selection of boxes, plastic tubs

1 Line the inside of a wok or bowl with food wrap, then cover with layers of newspaper soaked in PVA glue and water. Lift out your receiver dish when dry.

2 Poke 2 holes into the centre of the dish. Make 2 similar holes in the top half of a bottle. Thread wire through the dish and bottle, as shown. Twist the wire to secure. Paint the dish and cover the wire loop with a bottle top.

3 Make a radar pointer unit with bottle tops and a thin cardboard tube.

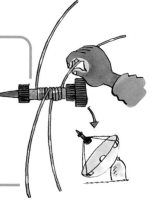

4 Wrap 4 long pieces of wire around the pointer unit to fix, then bend each one outwards to make spokes. Tape them to the sides of the dish.

5 Fix your radar to a platform made of tubes and boxes. Paint and decorate.

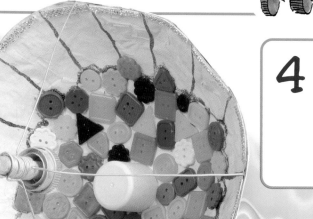

Can I make an accurate telescope?

When astronomers first viewed the night sky through telescopes, they were delighted with what they saw. But the images they enjoyed were always slightly fuzzy. Even with more powerful telescopes, they could not eliminate the blurring. If only clear pictures were possible.

Sir Isaac Newton designed the first reflecting telescope in 1668. His telescope used mirrors to reflect light rather than a lens to refract, or bend it.

The mirrors removed some of the blur caused by lenses. A flat mirror reflected light from a primary mirror to an eyepiece at the side of the telescope.

In 1672, a French scientist, Guillaume Cassegrain, designed a convex mirror that reflected the light through a hole in the main mirror to the eyepiece. It was an improvement, but still didn't cut out the slight blur.

Blurred images are so annoying! We must find a way to get really clear pictures of space.

WHAT DID THEY DO?

- In 1856, Justus von Liebig coated a reflector's mirror with silver, giving a more brilliant reflecting surface.

- During the 20th century, reflecting telescopes became bigger and bigger - from 1.5m at Mount Wilson to 5m at Mount Palomar - two observatories in California, USA.

- But reflecting telescopes, no matter how big, still can't produce a completely clear image. The Earth's atmosphere, which bends light, sees to that.

- Perhaps the answer lies beyond the Earth. Space flight is now more reliable and the shuttle can transport objects easily. It's worth a thought!

We'll use shuttle technology to take a special telescope into space. A space telescope orbiting Earth above the atmosphere will produce blur-free pictures. It will also include powerful X-ray and gamma ray telescopes.

The Hubble telescope orbits 600km above Earth, working round the clock to unlock the secrets of the universe.

Clear view

A **space telescope** operates beyond the atmosphere of the Earth. The Hubble Space Telescope was the first to be launched into **orbit**, in 1990, 610km above the Earth's surface. Its giant light-gathering mirror is 2.4m in diameter. Unfortunately, the mirror was flawed when the Hubble first went into space.

The pictures it sent back to Earth were out of focus. But in 1993, **astronauts** repaired the fault. The telescope now produces the most detailed images of objects in space ever seen on Earth. In fact, it can observe images 50 times fainter than any telescope on Earth can observe.

Black holes

A black hole is an invisible object with such a powerful gravitational pull that not even light can escape its surface. But if it's invisible and cannot be seen, how can scientists look for them? They use a special telescope – an x-ray telescope.

Astronomers have found that some objects in the universe give off most of their energy as x-rays. They find these objects using x-ray telescopes. These telescopes have iron and lead slats instead of mirrors. The slats block out all the x-rays except those from one line across the sky. These x-rays enter a gas-filled detector that absorbs them and counts them. The sources of x-rays can be found using the x-ray telescope to scan the sky. The brightest x-ray sources come from double stars, after one of them has collapsed. The collapsed star is called a **neutron star**, also known as a black hole. It can't be seen, but astronomers know it's there by the x-rays it gives off.

An x-ray telescope can 'see' where a black hole exists.

PIZZA MIRROR?

When telescope mirrors were first made, they were ground like lenses. But today, they are spin cast. A huge rotary oven spins the molten glass at a controlled speed, just like a pizza maker spins pizza dough. The spinning glass flows into a shape that is just right for a telescope mirror.

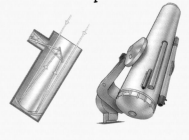

Inventor's words

astronaut
black hole
gravitational pull
neutron star
orbit
space telescope
x-ray telescope

Make a stargazy telescope

You will need

- scissors • card
- large, thick cardboard tube • toilet roll tubes
- 2 long nails
- sheet of acetate
- acrylic paint and brush
- narrow box
- 2 polystyrene cups
- double-sided tape
- PVA glue

1 Glue a card disc with a hole at the centre over one end of a large tube. Stick a toilet roll tube over the hole to make an eyepiece. Now push a nail through either side of the main body, as shown.

2 Cut out a disc of acetate to fit on the open end of the telescope. Paint starry patterns on the disc and glue the reverse side of it to the end.

3 Make a stand by glueing a thick wedge of card on either side of a narrow box.

4 Make 2 columns by glueing a cup to either side of 2 tubes.

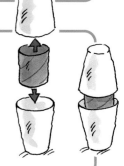

5 Push the 2 nails on the sides of the telescope through the top of the cup columns, and glue the bottoms to the stand. Paint and decorate.

Tilt your telescope towards the light for a starry view

How can I learn more about stars?

Astronomers are always finding new objects in space. Some are found by looking through a telescope; others are discovered by gathering radio or other waves. Telescopes gather light waves to produce images, but this tells only part of the story.

Astronauts in space can carry out experiments to find out what particles there are around stars or planets, or how much light is coming from them.

But it's not as good as actually being on the star or planet itself.

When astronauts walked on the Moon, they did experiments to find out what it is made of. But now, scientists also want to know what the stars and planets are composed of.

How can we possibly tell what a star is made of if we can't get there?

WHAT DID THEY FIND OUT?

- Scientists discovered that substances, like carbon, which are made of the same atoms, give off light if they are heated to a high enough temperature.

- They know that light can be split into electromagnetic waves of different lengths, which are different colours. This is called a spectrum.

- All atoms of an element give off large amounts of radiation at certain wavelengths. So the spectrum of that element's light has very bright lines at those particular wavelengths.

- Each element has its own special pattern of these bright lines, which is different from any other element. Will the lines tell us the rest of the story?

We'll develop a device that collects light from the stars, like a telescope. The device can divide the light into a spectrum. If the spectrum is analysed for its bright lines, we'll be able to tell from which elements the star is made.

Scientists check the Thermal Emission Imaging System (THEMIS) on board the Mars Odyssey Orbiter. THEMIS uses an infrared imaging spectrometer to map the Martian landscape.

Starlight

A **spectrograph** is an instrument used for breaking down light, usually from a star, into a **spectrum**. The spectrum can be recorded using a camera or a **charge-coupled device**, a type of electronic camera that gives clearer pictures than an ordinary one. It may also have a telescope for visual observation. A spectrograph is enclosed in a container.

This keeps out unwanted light. The light to be analysed enters through a slit and passes through a special lens to become parallel rays. These rays pass through a prism where the light is split into a spectrum. Another lens focuses the spectrum light on the exit slit. The spectrum is then analysed on film to decide what the star is made of.

Spectroscopy

Astronomers observe and analyse light to tell them more about objects in space, such as stars and dust clouds. Analysing light is called spectroscopy.

Spectroscopy uses a spectrograph for breaking up white light, the light that comes from the Sun and other sources, into individual wavelengths and their colours. The range of colours is called a spectrum. Spectroscopy can also be used to break up other types of radiation, such as gamma rays, or infra-red rays, into individual wavelengths. Spectroscopy can identify the types of atoms that make up a star's gaseous outer layer. It can also identify the **molecules** in the atmosphere of a planet. Astronomers sometimes use spectroscopy to determine the movements of stars or planets.

The dark lines in this spectrum show which types of light a star has absorbed. This indicates which elements the star contains.

X-RAY SPECTRUM

When scientists want to study an old supernova, they use an x-ray spectrograph. That's because it analyses x-rays from hot, highly energetic objects. The individual x-ray wavelengths create an x-ray spectrum that can be analysed to tell astronomers what the supernova is made of.

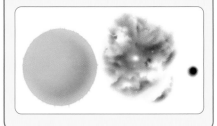

Inventor's words

charge-coupled device
molecule
spectrograph
spectroscopy
spectrum
supernova

Make a spectrum visor

You will need

- scissors • craft knife
- medium-sized shallow box • acetate
- 2 polystyrene cups
- coloured sweet papers
- corrugated card, metallic tape, sparkly pipe cleaners, sequins
- rigid plastic food tray large enough to fit over your eyes and nose
- long piece of thick elastic • cane • PVA glue
- paints and brush

1 Cut opposite ends out of the box. Then cut out windows on all 4 sides.

2 Cut out acetate squares and stick them over the windows.

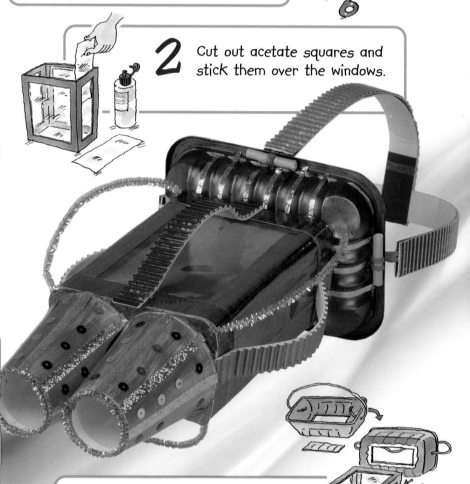

3 Cut the bottoms off 2 cups, stick on coloured sweet papers and glue the cups to one end of the window box, as shown. Decorate the eye-pieces with sparkly pipe-cleaners and sequins.

4 Cut a window out of the bottom of the tray and make holes at either side. Next thread through some elastic so you can strap the mask to your head (or you can attach card straps as shown).

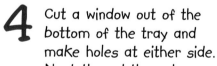

5 Glue the goggles onto the front of the plastic mask and decorate with corrugated board.

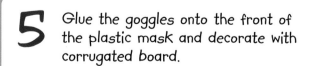

Glossary and index

MMU Manned manoeuvring unit. It is a jet-propelled backpack used by astronauts on space walks. p.18

Molecule Small particle containing two or more atoms that are joined together. A molecule of water has two atoms of hydrogen and one atom of oxygen. p.30, 42

Moon Earth's only natural satellite. It is the brightest object in the night sky. p.21

Multi-stage rocket Rocket with more than one rocket engine. The engines are arranged one above the other, with the lowest firing first and the others firing in turn. p.9

Neutron star Star that is mostly made up of neutrons. It forms after a supernova explosion. p.38

Orbit Path taken around a planet or other body by a natural or artificial object in space p.5, 22, 26, 37

Orbiter Manned part of a space shuttle. It sits on top of a large cigar-shaped fuel tank on take off. p.29

Outer space Anywhere beyond about 95km above the Earth's surface. p.14

Oxidiser Rocket engines carry oxygen in the form of an oxidiser. The oxidiser is mixed with the fuel in the combustion chamber. p.10

Payload bay Part of a space shuttle that carries the equipment to be used on a mission. p.30

Polar orbit Orbit that passes over the north and south poles. It always crosses the Equator at the same time of day. p.6

Propellant Liquid or solid fuel mix used to power a rocket. p.9

Pulsar Star which is a source of radio signals from space. p.34

Quasar Short for 'quasi-stellar radio source'. Quasars are galaxies which are far out in space. They send out strong visible light and strong radio signals. p.34

Radio spectrum Band of colour made when a beam of electromagnetic radiation splits into different wavelengths. Each colour corresponds to a wavelength. p.33

Radio telescope Device for collecting radio signals from space. Most have a dish antenna which can be turned in any direction towards any part of space. An amplifier and a detector are connected to the antenna. p.33

Rocket Powerful engine that uses a mixture of fuel and oxygen to produce gas at high pressure. The gas is expelled with a great force that thrusts the engine forward. A spacecraft that uses this type of engine is also called a rocket. p.12

Rocket fuel Special mixture of chemicals that are burned in a combustion chamber. p.10

Solar system System of planets orbiting a star or the Sun. p.25

Space Anywhere beyond our atmosphere. p.13

Space capsule Small pressurised cabin found in early US spacecraft. p.13

Space probe Unmanned space flight. Probes carry out missions to find out about moons, planets and other objects in the solar system. p.25

Space shuttle Spacecraft built by the United States of America. It can be reused many times, unlike three stage rockets. Space shuttles are launched like rockets, but they can land, like an aircraft, on a runway. p.29

Space suit Double garment worn by astronauts. The outer covering of the space suit protects the astronaut from harmful radiation and from space particles. The undersuit, or inner suit, contains the heating and cooling systems that protect against very hot or very cold temperatures. p.17

Space telescope Telescope that operates in space beyond the atmosphere of the Earth. p.37

Spectrograph Instrument used for breaking down light, usually from a star, into a spectrum. p.41

Spectroscopy Analysis, by scientists, of light. Astronomers observe and analyse light to find out more about objects in space such as stars and dust clouds. p.42

Spectrum Band of colours made when a beam of electromagnetic radiation is split into its different wavelengths. Each colour of the spectrum corresponds to a wavelength. p.41

Splash theory Theory that suggests that Earth was hit early in its history by a huge object. Material splashed out from the Earth's molten surface and creates a ring around it. The debris of the ring then coalesced, or joined together, to create the Moon. p.22

Supernova Star that has exploded. Supernovas happen when very large, old stars run out of nuclear fuel and collapse inwards. p.34, 42

Undersuit Inner suit of a space suit that contains the heating and cooling systems, which protect against very hot or very cold temperatures. p.17

X-ray telescope Telescope used to find objects such as black holes that seem to be invisible. X-ray telescopes have iron and lead slats instead of mirrors. The slats block out all the X-rays except those from one line across the sky. These X-rays enter a gas filled detector that absorbs them and counts them. p.38

Tools and Materials

Almost all of the materials in this book can be found around the house or bought at your local art or craft shop. If you cannot find the exact item, try and replace it with something similar.

Most of the models will stick fast with PVA glue or even wallpaper paste. However, some materials need a stronger glue so take care when using these as they may damage your clothes and even your skin. Ask an adult to help you.

Always cover furniture with newspaper or a large cloth, and protect your clothes by wearing a work apron.

User Care

Take special care when handling sharp tools such as scissors, pointed gadgets, pieces of wire or craft knives. Ask an adult to help you when you need to use them.